for Andrew and Peter,
who have their own
stories to tell. —S. K.

to George Nuttal Gordon
for bringing his stories
to my world. —J. R.

Anansi Takes a Challenge

Long ago the first spider,

Kwaku Anansi,

lived in Africa.

He swung on his webs

from tree to tree

or ran on his thin legs

along the ground.

ANANSI
AND THE
BOX OF STORIES

A WEST AFRICAN FOLKTALE

ADAPTED BY **STEPHEN KRENSKY**
ILLUSTRATED BY **JENI REEVES**

M Millbrook Press/Minneapolis

The illustrator thanks models Leroy V, Leroy VI, and Carmen Square; Artie Henderson and Artie Henderson Jr.; and Stuart Reeves. Thanks also to Robert L. Jeanne, Department of Entomology, University of Wisconsin, and James M. Carpenter, Curator of Hymenoptera, American Museum of Natural History, for their expertise in tracking down the wasp Polybioides. And thanks to Susan Kuecker, curator of the African American Museum of Cedar Rapids, Iowa, and the Blank Park Zoo of Des Moines, Iowa.

Millbrook Press
A division of Lerner Publishing Group, Inc.
241 First Avenue North
Minneapolis, MN 55401 U.S.A.

Website address: www.lernerbooks.com

Library of Congress Cataloging-in-Publication Data

Krensky, Stephen.
    Anansi and the box of stories / adapted by Stephen Krensky ; illustrations by Jeni Reeves.
        p. cm. — (On my own folklore)
    Summary: Long ago in Africa, the sky god Nyame keeps all of the stories to himself, but when Anansi the spider asks their price, Nyame agrees to trade his stories if Anansi can perform four seemingly impossible tasks.
    ISBN: 978-0-8225-6741-7 (lib. bdg. : alk. paper)
    1. Anansi (Legendary character) —Legends. [1. Anansi (Legendary character) — Legends. 2. Folklore—Africa, West.] I. Reeves, Jeni, ill. II. Title.
PZ8.1.K8663Anb 2008
398.2—dc22   2006037783

Manufactured in the United States of America
5 – RRD – 5/15/13

In that distant time,
no one told stories on Earth.
Why? No one had any to tell.
The sky god, Nyame,
kept them all to himself
up in his sky kingdom.

5

The stories told of happiness and sadness
and the mysteries of the world.
Many creatures asked Nyame
to share the stories.
But the sky god refused.
Anansi was curious about the stories too.
So he went to see Nyame.
The sky god waved him away
"You are only a spidery old man.
How will you ever pay for my stories?"
Anansi knew better than to argue
with the sky god.
"I only wish to know the price," he said.
"I don't yet know if I can pay it."

Nyame laughed again.

"Very well. I will trade my stories
for four fierce animals.
First is the python Onini,
the snake that swallows people up.
Second is Mmoboro,
the hornets that buzz and sting.
Third is Osebo, the leopard
whose teeth are as sharp as knives.
And fourth is the fairy Mmoatia,
who stays unseen as the wind.
"That is a high price," said Anansi.
"Such stories must be wonderful indeed."
Then he bowed and returned to Earth.

When Anansi got home,
he told his wife, Aso,
what Nyame had said.
"I am no match for these creatures
in strength or speed," Anansi said.
"How can I capture Onini?
If I make a mistake,
he will surely swallow me."

"A python's strength lies in its body,
not its brain," said Aso.
"You must outsmart him from the start."
She paused.
"To do this, you will need
a palm branch
and some long vines."
Then she explained the rest of the plan.

11

Anansi took the branch and the vines
to the stream near where Onini lived.
"Onini is a great python,"
Anansi said loudly.
"I'm sure he is longer than this branch."

Onini listened from the leafy shadows,
and Anansi's words confused him.
So he slithered out onto the path.
"What's that you were saying, spider?"
the python asked.

"I was talking about you," Anansi said.

"You see this branch?

My wife, Aso, said that it was longer

than you are.

I told her she was wrong.

This branch could not be longer

than the greatest snake in the world.

But my wife is very stubborn.

She said I should come see you
and find out once and for all."
"Put the branch next to me,"
said Onini. "I will stretch out
to my full length.
Then we will see who is telling the truth."
Anansi put down the palm branch,
and Onini leaned against it.

"Well?" Onini asked.

"Patience," said Anansi.

"I must measure carefully."

As he talked, he bound the python
to the branch with the long vines.

Over and over,
he wound them around.

"So what have you learned?"
Onini asked at last.

"Good news!" said Anansi.

"I was right. You are a little longer."

Onini was as pleased as the greatest snake
in the world could be.

"So now you can release me," he said.

"I wish that I could," said Anansi.
"But there is also bad news.
I must take you to Nyame."
So Anansi spun a web around Onini
and carried him back to the sky god.

If Nyame was surprised
to see Onini, he hid it well.
"I will take the python,"
he said to Anansi.
"But you are not done yet."

19

Mmoboro the Hornets

Anansi returned home
to share the news with Aso.
"All is well," she said.
"And yet your face is long."
"What can I do about Mmoboro?"
Anansi asked his wife.
"I cannot wrap them in vines."

Aso nodded.

"Hornets that buzz and sting

will slip through even nimble fingers.

But hornets are nervous

and quick to worry.

First, you must fill an empty gourd

with water."

Anansi understood.

After he filled the gourd,

he went walking through the forest.

"Bzzzzzzzzzzzz."

Anansi heard Mmoboro buzzing overhead.

He climbed up a tree above them.

Then he sprinkled some water

from the gourd onto their nest.

The hornets buzzed louder.

"The rain is coming!

The rain is coming!

We will all get terribly wet!"

Anansi cut a large leaf from the tree
and held it over his head.
Then he took the rest of the water
and poured it over the leaf.
"The rain is falling," Anansi shouted,
as the water dripped around him.

"We know!" cried Mmoboro.

"But what can we do?"

"You are lucky I am here,"
said Anansi.

"If you come inside my gourd,
the rain will not reach you."

The hornets did not hesitate.
They flew right into the gourd.
When they were all inside,
Anansi plugged up the gourd
and spun a web around it.
"You will be very safe
from the rain now," he said.

Then he returned again
to Nyame in the sky kingdom
in the clouds.
The sky god took Mmoboro
as he had Onini.
"I will take the hornets," he said.
"But you are not done yet."

Osebo the Leopard

Again Anansi returned home.
"What can I do about Osebo?"
he asked his wife.
"I cannot wrap him in vines
or catch him in a gourd."
"And his teeth are as sharp as knives."
"It would be wise to keep him
at a safe distance," said Aso.
"You must start with a large hole."

Anansi nodded.

He knew what his wife meant,

as he had dug such holes before.

Anansi returned to the jungle

and found Osebo's tracks.

There he dug a deep hole.

Then he covered up the hole

with leaves, so it was hard to see.

The next morning,
Anansi returned to the hole.
Osebo was prowling around the bottom.
"What has happened here?"
Anansi asked.
Osebo growled at him,
showing teeth like knives.
"What do you think?
I did not see this hole in the darkness,
and I fell in."

"How unlucky," said Anansi.

"This should be a lesson to you

not to wander around in the dark."

"I do not care about lessons now,"

said Osebo.

"I care about getting out.

Whoever dug this hole

will return soon to take me away."

"Perhaps I can help," said Anansi.

"I see some long sticks here.

If I lower them down,

maybe you can climb up on them."

"Hurry!" said Osebo.

"We may not have much time."

So Anansi put down the sticks.

Osebo placed his paws on them.

"The sticks are wobbly," he complained.

"I am doing the best I can," said Anansi.

"You must stay low and hold on tight."

Osebo crept up the sticks,
keeping his head down.
But when he was almost out,
Anansi hit him over the head
with a club.

Osebo groaned.

Quickly, Anansi spun

his strongest web string

around the leopard and the sticks.

"What are you doing?" Osebo roared.

"This is no escape!"

"True enough," Anansi admitted.

"For I must take you to Nyame."

Anansi returned to the sky god.

Nyame was not surprised to see him.

"I will take the leopard," he said.

"But you are not done yet."

Mmoatia the Fairy

Anansi was happy he had captured

three of Nyame's creatures.

But how would he ever capture Mmoatia?

"How do I find a fairy who is invisible?"

he asked Aso.

"You cannot find her," Aso said.

"You must make her find you."

Anansi started by carving a wooden doll.

When he was finished,

the doll looked almost real.

Anansi covered it

with sticky gum from a plant.

Anansi took the doll to the odum tree,
where he knew the fairies played.
He then pounded some yams in a bowl
until they became a tasty paste.
He put the bowl in the doll's lap.
Then Anansi tied a vine to the doll's neck
and went off to hide in the bushes.

Before long, Mmoatia came by.
She saw the doll sitting alone
under the odum tree.
She also noticed the pounded yams.
"May I have some of your food?"
she asked hungrily.

Anansi pulled on the vine
he had tied to the doll's neck.
The doll nodded.
Mmoatia started eating and eating.
Soon the bowl was empty.
She wiped her mouth and stood up.
"Thank you," she said to the doll.

The doll said nothing.

"I said thank you," Mmoatia said again.

The doll remained silent.

"Where are your manners?"
asked Mmoatia.

"I have thanked you twice.
And you will not answer.
This is no way to behave.
You need to be taught a lesson."

43

Mmoatia grabbed the doll's shoulder.

She tried to pull her hand away,

but it was held tight.

She grabbed the doll with her other hand.

SPLAT!

Now Mmoatia was really mad.

She kicked the doll with one foot

and then the other.

Both were then stuck as well.

Anansi stepped out
from the bushes.
"What have we here?" he asked.
Mmoatia vanished at once, but that did no good.
Visible or not, her hands and feet
were still stuck tight to the doll.

45

So Anansi spun a web
around Mmoatia and brought
her up to Nyame.
When the sky god saw them,
he called together everyone in the kingdom.
"Hear me," he told them.
"Anansi has met my price.
My stories are now his
to do with as he pleases."

When Anansi got home,
he shared the stories with Aso.
They laughed and cried
and even shouted in surprise
at the endings.
But they did not keep
the stories to themselves.
They told them to others
and still do to this day.

Afterword

Anansi is one of the most important figures in West African folklore. His story began long ago with the Ashanti people of Ghana. The Ashanti belong to a larger group called the Akan. Tales about Anansi spread to other West African regions. They then spread to islands in the Caribbean Sea and to North and South America.

In some stories, Anansi is a spider. Sometimes he is a man who can climb and spin webs like a spider. But in all stories, Anansi is a trickster. A trickster is a character who uses tricks to do certain tasks. Tricksters also like to break the rules set by the gods or by nature. A trickster can be a good or a bad character. Anansi uses his tricks to do something good. He brings stories to Earth so that all creatures can enjoy them.

Other parts of *Anansi and the Box of Stories* are taken from Akan and Ashanti culture and folklore. For example, the fairy Mmoatia has backwards feet, as fairies do in West African tales. And the sky god, Nyame, wears kente cloth. Kente is a brightly colored cloth traditionally woven and worn by the Ashanti.

To learn more about Anansi and African folklore, see *Timeless Tales of Anansi* by Nathaniel Hosea Ormsby, *Tiger Soup: An Anansi Story from Jamaica* by Frances Temple, and *A Pride of African Tales* by Donna L. Washington.